The Book of a Hundred Hands

KUHL HOUSE POETS *edited by Jorie Graham and Mark Levine*

The Book of a Hundred Hands

POEMS BY COLE SWENSEN

UNIVERSITY OF IOWA PRESS IOWA CITY

University of Iowa Press, Iowa City 52242
http://www.uiowa.edu/uiowapress

Printed in the United States of America

The University of Iowa Press is a member of Green Press Initiative and is committed to preserving natural resources.

Printed on acid-free paper

Library of Congress Cataloging-in-Publication Data
Swensen, Cole.
The book of a hundred hands: poems / by Cole Swensen.
p. cm.—(Kuhl House poets)
ISBN 0-87745-946-0 (pbk.)
1. Hand—Poetry. I. Title. II. Series.
PS3569.W384B66 2005
811'.54—dc22 2004065651

05 06 07 08 09 P 5 4 3 2 1

for Claude Royet-Journoud

Contents

Acknowledgments

The author would like to thank the editors and staffs of the following journals for their generous support in publishing these poems, in some cases, in earlier versions and/or under altered or different titles.

Bellingham Review: "The Hand as Origami"
Chicago Review: "The Hand Sculpted," "The Hand Sketched"
Colorado Review: "Traveling," "The Hand as Anchor," "Sigh"
Columbia Poetry Review: "Intro to the Palmar View," "Fingers 1," "Fingers 2"
Conjunctions: "The History of the Hand," "The Prehistory of the Hand," "The Hand Thinks," "The Hand Defined: 1," "Grasp," "Fan," "Hold"
Conundrum: "Chirologia," "Case Histories"
Facture 4: "The Hand Etched in Glass," "The Mechanics of the Hand," "The Hand as Window"
Fourteen Hills: "Fingertips," "The Hand: Other Arches"
Harvard Review: "The Hands' Testament," "The Hand as Historical"
The Iowa Review: "Shadow Puppets"
No: "Knuckles," "The Thumb, in Sum"
Now Culture: "The Hand as Ideogram," "The Hand as Lamp,"
QSQ: "The Palmar View"
Shiny: "The Hand as Mansion," "The Hand as Stair"
Ur-Vox: "Marc Chagall," "Marcel Duchamp," "Rembrandt van Rijn," "Norman Bluhm and Frank O'Hara"
Verse: "The Hands Testify," "The Hand Painted In"
Volt: "The Hand in Fresco," "Juggle"
Word/For Word: "The Hand That Caresses," "The Hand as Harbor"

I would also like to thank a+bend Press, which published an earlier version of section four as a chapbook titled *And Hand*.

The title and much of the anatomical information in section five comes from *The Book of a Hundred Hands* by George B. Bridgman (Dover, 1971). *The Hand* by Frank R.

Wilson (Vintage, 1998) was also extremely helpful as well as simply fascinating, and supplied the quotation that opens the poem "Case Histories." The seventeenth-century references were found in *Imagining Language*, edited by Steve McCaffery and Jed Rasula (MIT Press, 1998), and the italicized line in "The Hand That Caresses" is taken from Alphonso Lingis's *The Community of Those Who Have Nothing in Common* (Indiana University Press, 1994). And thanks to Jena Osman for showing me *A Manual of Gesture* by Albert M. Bacon, 1879, on which section eight is based. Warm thanks to Susan Gevirtz for showing it to me and saying, "You should write a book about it."

If you do know that *here is one hand*, we'll grant you all the rest.

—Wittgenstein, *On Certainty*

ONE The History of the Hand

THE HISTORY OF THE HAND

Once thistle, once fissure, once a lamp in fog
and so on

Once convinced, we agreed to hold
which used to mean to anoint before it meant to bless
or lessen
or whiten the sky

"Hands appear in the earliest" (framed, sized) and overflowing the margins, the man born with two left hands was born a grown man.
The man born with his hands full of hands later died. There's no mystery to this. You listen, looking down, counting, thinking *And*?

Assyrian hands were carved of stone.
Egyptian hands were the point of the tale.
The Gothic hand, like no other, launched, while that of the Renaissance, both early and late, fragile and breaks, a wave on light. Ghirlandaio had hands of willow, and every hand that Dürer ever drew thrived. Most hands are startlingly small, like eyes.

THE PREHISTORY OF THE HAND

The hand began an animal, and from thereon filled

some folded mile, that soft
plural kite
in flock did herd
who thus did shard
comes to mind first
you will note the exploded stasis used to mean star
or halt
in every native language
you hold it straight out. Stark. Startle. Harp.
When you hold out your hand and the whole world stops and you find yourself
looking at the back of your hand, which, the longer you look at it, looks starved.

THE HAND THINKS

There's a hand that thinks, that lies inside, that lines the hand that moves

and it thinks: "While tying a knot, you can utterly forget, you can think
(can be thinking of something else at the time)
that muscles have a memory all their own
that lives again a braided time
alive
I tie.

Watch
what without you lives. The life of fingers
harbors
mutiny that doesn't even bother. The hand, ever prior
avatar of architecture: archlessly, each one

is a frame.
There's an empty frame on the wall and the hand is the sky
that opens the wall.

THE HAND DEFINED: I

As with any word, where does it begin? an elbowful of muscle fine as an inner ear

Those who say the definition of the hand begins in the shoulder say those who say between
and 4.2 million years ago, *Australopithecus anamemsis*: To find. Fossils of the hands and feet
so much rarer than those of skulls. Filed down to filigree

a brittle hearing

with the fingertips all those singly, millions

of early braille, caressing an armful of dirt as they fell

are falling still

entire

systems in the back and shoulders

and enormous parts of the brain.

THE HAND DEFINED: 2

As what will not relent: The felting delta mapped in the mind

with its boundless arboretum of neural withins:

the witness: to insist it

is equally infinite out there in its fingers

a port city in a blizzard.

THE HAND DEFINED: 3

A hand is anything that augments,
is the exponent of its own extent.
Look again. Nothing looks stranger
than a hand after time, its several failures sequential, enabled and
hold that wronged
until it's just that much
fish-hook,
borealis,
and/or burial mound   come other   unto some
not yet arrived. Can meanwhile
calibrate a fly, my alluvial spire.

CHIROLOGIA, OR THE NATURAL LANGUAGE OF THE HAND

after John Bulwer, 1644

That He appeared unto Him

and asked what do you have in your hand

precedes thought,
was thought to abide within
this gift

is the sign, alit, and thus aligned, and thus which tide
will twin? Much less graceful, then, is the clumsy tongue,
that shapeless intention devoid of self-difference, compared to the dexterous
multitude of poise: fingular fan on table

chair

or cheekbone, speak volumes
into voiceless air, *the gesture*

(We seek forbearance) (Watch our patience)
against all excess of ideation (the hand is pacing).

(The hand — by its very nature, a thing in the world,
a worldly thing, a veritable map (or planet or lens) — note: even in its shape, its marvelous extent, which each time it flexes, expands, becomes an increasing part, a dominant trend, and so (fewer and fewer can now be spoken) silent that it cannot help but see: feather : feature : words when early

are bone

said the boneman,

unsaid, said the

one among

the fled.

OF AN ALPHABET OF STEPPES

after the finger alphabet of George Dalgarno, 1680

But after he was gone, I began to consider
that the "I" floats above the middle finger
                                        and the deaf with their kites
and the "O" above the next
                                        who touched
the "E" above the index — note
it's the vowels that live in air
and the continents distributed
rationally across extremity.
                                        Readiness
                                        is distillation
                                        among strangers.

Helvetius, 1758, when writing on the mind, says, for example, wrists, or man would have wandered, for example, islands at the ends of the arms, among the animals, is defenseless and depictions of the hand began with thousands of fingers, then hundreds, then ten, then how have we come to this who once wandered confusing stars.

Just walk on in
and you end:
Arch, and the window flies open; splay, and the house falls down.
Streets that seem silent only now.
Walk on (says a voice at your spine). Light the lamps that hang. The light is long
and swings from
what lines an avenue? and
what had to change to make that shine?
or that one run?
and at every corner, an ark on fire — a hand and its menagerie, visible for miles.

THE HAND AS HISTORICAL

A fossil hides time — and thus hides from itself, that else
is the human compass
is the hand — and sows
                    a composite home, its only hour,
and that, in fact, the graph
is a palm — just look what falls within
                              (and lands, it's said, and knows its way) was day
                              before the latter was invented — all is lost
                              it's said: what spine is this? or better put, what animal
with five spines. (Who survived?) A fossil is a photograph of chance.

A HISTORY OF THE HAND

Skip a stone across a water. Your eye will unfurl you, counting
and counted on whoever also

learned the names (then matched them

to a face or other lighted surface). What do you have in your

You'd think that now, with all this space within, they'd be less empty now

you'll remember

them all.

TWO Positions of the Hand

GRASP

As the hand carved first its arc in air, a corresponding sweep through the brain
made aviary spaces a little like airplane hangars in their relative dimensions
and thus the impression
of standing under a sky you can see.
                                        The supple wrist, as it turned, turned too in the mind
and acquired

all we can do, for instance, with the thumb and a single finger.
What can you remember doing first thing this morning
among the answers and the liquid trees
                                                    Who picked this fruit
                                                    of
                                                    just
the key in the door got there by itself. The lights just grew on the trees.

FAN

Species of when, that outward cliff
heart-shaped under everything left. It was a compliment:
the hands of a surgeon or those of a gift. It was hot that summer
and every day thereafter

gripped the sleeves. The vanes of a fan are often made
from bone she said I own this one
of painted air paired
where air spears
and folds into ribs turned to leaves turned to hands,
those veils that arrange the face. Summer gate. Sun made of gave.

GRIP

The intricate isthmus of the wrist made initial

right below the skin, its glazed mosaic cradles
                                                                                                                                              a glint

as the hand swings down, we hear a slight clock and another era finds

radial and *ulnar* and deviant
                                                                                continental plates that drift
                                                                                into place. It took a million years
to pick up a hammer or a cane,
and each time you do you
forget another million years.

HOLD

The cup the hand becomes

a bell

is first a shape,
and then there's something old in your hand.
The held being
a function of the inverted arch
and ease of vault when looking up, an immense

Walk backwards from here to the sea

until serial, this shell

is what surrounds, is all that might be
the connection between tool use, language, and the spiral gene determining
twenty-one muscles set out to sea
on a perfectly lovely day.
The hand is a boatless sail.

SIGH

You pass your hand over your eyes.
There are two ways to do this – palm in or palm out. Try it. Pass
your hand over your eyes first with the palm facing out (you're tired, my

then
with the palm facing in, the hand can barely pass, is too exact; it clicks
in traces
to bitter palace

to stay

means siege
you say,
throwing back your head. You could be acting. We
could be watching you from the other side; you
could have forgotten that.

JUGGLE

The sky is the constant, and against it slides a planet
is anything that moves
across
we look all arc.
(I practice each trick
behind a curtain where it's warm
eye : hand   hand : calibration through
a practiced "We
tend to forget what the hand cannot do without." "I see
each move clearly in my mind,
and it's fine."   Look away.   Carry
the brimming teacup across the crowded station. Watch
my hands. Said the multitude: Memory
is every muscle's sovereignty; eternity is a thumb.

TRAVELING

As it carves its world
from the aerodrome of nerve and dream, additional dimensions and projections
of the thing, enormous, internal
and verdant
becomes this
                    acreage paced, this mile after mile
that the hand each day travels as it waves,
or covers a yawn, or sweeps, or puts down
a baton. The orchestra conductor wears an odometer
instead of a watch.

GLOVE

Wore the middle ghost.
Click of needle-on-sun
                                        who runs
out ahead of the oncoming

who runs out into

forest after forest,
the lamp on the table
that fits.

THE MECHANICS OF THE HAND

Some natural ways it lies, for instance on a desk, are due
not so much to mental states as to the mechanics of the hand.
Locked in.
While your face was taught
to hold itself, the hands, electric, spread. While speaking always stands outside,
instinctive means it angles toward
the natural inheritance of all beautiful things: balance,
precision, and extremes: These
innate positions including
(in adversity)
a wholly involuntary outward mobility
(the whole body tends to move out
of limb and feature —
Picture
A woman fleeing a burning building
A man with his hands on fire

The basal knuckles are always more likely
to bend forward. We close in, understanding
like phantom pain
can lodge itself in any finger and wait.

THREE Professions of the Hand

CASE HISTORIES: PHYSICAL APHASIA

"We can't be sure what the child, though watched,
was really doing with his hands . . ."

and the next phrase is
"before he was"

there are
enormous gaps in the planet — they usually occur

in the vast

sense of touch, so often

fields. The

lifted sense.
The sixth What are you doing
expects to be empty, or oceans. Now they've got oceans

And the child reached with the half that saw
and touched half a giving saved
some image that walks through walls and owns this older orbit
flailing sheaves.

Can cause a street;
it's from the shape — held straight up, you can't help but see.
            And those who have chosen to live in the dark, equally happily
the hand burns on:
Whole forests bequeath:
                        Lantern! Lantern!
gone all out of range

And we who believe in cause and effect,
                                    whose trees thrive in the falling sun,
should learn a little more about fire,
which I hear is not hard to do.

THE HAND AS ANCHOR

Raked sun.
Or there did it lodge. Or rock. Or did it stone? It to stone. The scarred just
that yet insists:
follow this
who still believes
the architecture of a ship
is derived from that of the human body or perhaps only the hand
caught, and the whole body stopped. It's a shame.

THE HAND THAT CARESSES

after Alphonso Lingis

Glean sheet
that's soft and flees
gliding just above the surface
constructs a second skin of close attention.
The hand cannot tire in the face

of another, a hand hovers or floats
detached from the wrist, my hand fits your face precisely *What recognizes the suffering of the other is a movement in one's hand.* He points to the plane, which is landing, which is the same.

THE HAND AS ORIGAMI

First Position: Crane
Second Position: Freighter. The winged lion comes later.
This is the church
and this is the people who

walked across a land bridge and ever since

however flesh, there's a turning in the bird,
a burning egg
I thin with sandpaper; that's land down there,
liminal.

THE HAND AS 19TH-CENTURY HARBOR

That would be the harbinger hand
                                        and so I'll stay here. And of the flocks
full forth on the gale, a hand is every one. Broke, and vague, and starfish
will, like a watermark on a letter, splay across the window. Don't say omen, there are too many ships. They are alight, and they write
vile things in the newspapers like
"All hands on deck" and "All hands were lost" and "Every hand
becomes a ghost, so do the math. It's a little hope. It means we outnumber them, until they outnumber us
forcing her eyes down the list in the morning paper.

THE THEATER OF THE HAND

Chart it on a staff, both the shape of the note and that of the hand
of the music therein. Marinetti wrote a play
composed entirely of hands
that waved above a sheet when the lights came on.

In another (whose?) a mime stood alone on stage
and when the lights went down, all that remained were his hands gloved
in something that glows in the dark. Such as will not spread in the dark

such as five years. Arrange them as you like.

THE HAND AS IDEOGRAM

In a dark purple sky behind the lightning field, alive
Michaux, *Later the signs spoke to me*
And they were hands

murmur without end

The hand is not human

and no word adheres

held out, half a million
that half-ended in bright migration. We once recognized them.

in which the panes infinitesimal. By the thousands, the armies of the ancient world
got older. A sweeping sensation mistaken for wind. You opened the window.
You thought that would do.
This is not so different from certain congenital conditions in which

You open the window. There is more you can see through. For instance, if the body
is 98% water and the window looks out on an ocean
is the hand in all its facets
a latch.

THE HAND AS MANSION

When you first walk in, all you see is the view — a huge sweep across rolling green with here and there a stand of cypress, outcroppings, single oaks, all in varied shades and endless under light, ridge, bird, ridge, and on the farthest ridge, though small at this distance, a huge white house with its turrets and wings and enormous windows so positioned that you look right through it.

THE HAND AS SUN GOD

The term “pillars of the wrist” was engraved upon the lintel
through which one enters
the deeply placed. We want the neural point.
There is a pause
in the curve that resists gravitation,
that suspends
a glass gyroscope on the windowsill; one has invisible friends
that turn on a central axis
like a revolving door,
hands are a form of wind.

THE HAND POLISHES

This is now uncommon. And therefore brittles:
To polish is to
raise the carapace, the doorknob, the letterbox, the concierge, who,
gleaming in the sun, turns to steer. This gilded bone. All things in which

Did not reflect our faces. Or those of any we knew.
This is a nameplate. Affixed
to a doorway. No, to a door. Answer: there's no one there.
This is decor; a thin layer of gold
that shines in tune. A leaf on which is added one to one and one.
It's a name "scratched"
"thereon"
if I raise
a finger and say I'm not at home, please; I may for once

Please show me home.

When gold leaf crumples, it disappears.
There's no one at the door, but we
told you this already, there is

the door.   The man who polishes it was born
with a missing hand. Whose?
he says, and laughs at the joke,
but we told you this already.

EXPRESSION

Where the bones form a scape

out there beyond the trees. Great wind will make the creases deeper. The tendons rise and the knuckles spread. A range of hills becomes the focus of involuntary waking dreams. Modern psychology tells us that it's modern, that it glows red when happy, that it exceeds itself.

THE HAND AS STAIRCASE

Or as sunlight on a stair
                    Follow the curve
across a brow. Later
a film still in which a Venetian blind, a streetlight outside,
and the face climbs,
one at a time, spiraling outward as the flight turns

we revert
to the brow. The shadows thrown by the streetlight
are not quite parallel, a city on a hill.

And how happy we are here! On a corner
about to cross the street and enter the park

at the top of the hill, from which you see the tops of dozens of hills.

THE HAND AS NEST

What caress?

and who

of slate who made

this flute, you

hollow out a bone with a smaller bone.

You choose a fruit the size and shape of a heart.

THE HAND AS MANGO

Rounded the corner, and I always bet
on horses in alphabetical order. Take it home
to light the corridor, or carry it with you,
just slip it in your pocket. You have no home.

FOUR Representations of the Hand

THE HANDS' TESTAMENT

The face veils and gates
and the glance will enharbor,

but the thumb and forefinger
could give it away entire

but will never

but remain, calmly clasped
and "therein lies." It's light out. And I, nearer

No, you knew what inner

We have many versions

that require silence

differs less than one percent
                    (I rest my case)
                    (as I was blessed)
                    it is
the shimmer in the hybrid; the hand is an island
oddly endless; we are it.

THE HANDS TESTIFY

As if the sun had hit

the glazing

slips
as if

there are days it all goes right

for instance:
There's a greenhouse just out of sight.
All I can see is a greenhouse, the glass in the sun, the green
is somewhere else. The hand arches over
the head of the child and floats down. The hand is planned
as a perfect inversion of the head. Child and mine, a building of eyes. You can see
through the hand or think you can
to the flower of the brain, but all along it's the hand
that's blooming, and the child is incidental, or at least not central to the scene.

THE HAND PAINTED IN

Is said is unhinged   can drift off from   is not constrained to

Though the hand, as if tethered, often stays in place
                                        the great painters could aloft each cell
where the living shifts into distance while we, the living, devise new methods:
You grind down a lightbulb and paint in the hands. This, said the Renaissance, shall,
in that required posture, cause them to stutter
                                                  to flicker
                                                  to rise on will. The hand is yet
one more instance of the incantation of the awkward god of uneven number, of
all knuckle, El Greco, my own Elba,
                                          and all the in-between that glows in the dark. Arc-
en-ciel, or carved boat, or matching boats like the blue hands that saints often wear.

Gets huge. Multiplies the bone. Here, too, the sun is fundamental; it overflows and joins
the vagrant rays and you say, oh yes,
that one.   Stronger in effort, my pyred posture
arrives between sky and sky, a lithe difference I wish
upon all indestructible things this freak wing.

THE HAND ETCHED IN GLASS

We knew this was coming. We always thought they were flying, but, no, it's light alone. It's morning and the light is streaming in. Blinding, you think, and put your hand up to your eyes. And stayed. We're all part window. There's someone coming in through the french window, but you don't notice him; you notice the window.

> And you wonder why the pane was made; such tracery, cf. antiquity, or it could be simply in the distance. We've always thought We're all a part
>
> streaming in in the background glass gets articulate

And you wonder why the pane was made, and you look at the pane, not at him.

THE HAND SKETCHED

By nature, will feather in disjointture

                                                            will beckon

to be the last surviving of a surviving

troupe of tangents with fog in the distance,
with a stand of trees on a ridge penciled in
that far away, it gains
a healing force. Thus is the hand

                                                  sealed in its swift expanse,

                                        and thus impossible to photograph

until quite recently, an incandescent flare orbiting an end.

THE HAND PHOTOGRAPHED

Here we tend toward particulars, though we remain black & white and/or the black before the door, the white, slipping out. We're more angular than their portraits would have led you to believe; you could live here too — we're not as poor as we look. Photographs have a way of implying that it was a little cold that day, or that we live like pets in the laps of everyone who wanted something else.

THE HAND IN FRESCO

Behind the glass block wall there walks

Put roses behind the glass block window, red ones, it's hard to tell
just what's going on. There are saints coming down. And tribes
that turn to chalk when the photograph strikes. He put up his hand
to protect his face and the hand remained.

You can make it into a wall. All these colors into pale
to whisper: "Wilt silt,
                    wilt sift.
Sieve.
You can see through me. I'm the one wearing ice. I have crossed
my hands behind.

FIVE The Anatomy of the Hand

INTRO TO THE PALMAR VIEW

The hand that is not a small world —
flexor, fascia, and fibrous expansion;
                                        from the condyle of the humerus comes
and over the annular ligament does   at the gates of
                                        (hold this)
                    and the opponens muscles of the thumb. Some
dumb piano, summer drones on. Palms
and the calluses of the palm, the upper plains, ingrained,
                              and to this extent
              its eminence
passes over,
ends in
the ability to fold a newspaper on a moving train.

THE PALMAR VIEW

Here the hand is usually bent;
if at the wrist, a chiseled arc   angles to an eventual   middle finger
is another dark
they say
is most often the most often curved. Darkness makes things
turn on their own. I'm sure you've seen. The index and the little finger are,
on the other hand, the most extreme. Things that have a light in them,
things that spring up and out and seem to hold, hold on. These include
small undercuts where shadows collect among the awake.

There are four bones. There are fingers toward. They are fastened to the inner. There is something called interossei; we have them. Dorsal almost everywhere and when you draw in. We learned that from. Watch closely the animals; some move outward; these are called spreaders. They “draw away”; they lie deep, they.

PALMAR 3

Already interior, this is landscape this vast of veld,
this escapes, and lintel crossed

left a letter in the dust, or
as it settles, sifting through the tendons
in their numbered positions
and innumerable interstices
rising up from the sea, lonely but determined.

FINGERS 1

Lattice into swallow, the fingers built in shallows; they are beyond
and so the creases do not penetrate. They are beyond. Enclosed
in differing lengths. Bevel. Apex of the knuckle, which
point it never reaches, there being others farther on.

FINGERS 2

All belongs with them:
the plural oar the fingers when straight
really are all that palm extrapolate of frond
a portion henged
my friend goes
toward the many and the several
that geometric engine
that spelled in space
the constellation crane or ibis or heron in its length to depth ratio
of one of those
things that makes you say
how on earth do they stand or how do they fly or some small unlikely
anger of bones.

FINGERS: ALIGNMENT

We of the congregation do declare the constellation

I'm blind; I've always known it, but never before has it
complied.

I think of the people I see every day, and then of the people I see
four or five days a week. And then those I see twice,
and then once. And then I know no one,

and suddenly it's crowded, integral, and just what I'd imagined
I knew
any section of sky. Maps
of the sky date back to
etc. I'm blind, thus
I see with my hands, thus.

Radiate that splay
from the strangely pulseless point
                                        makes an isosceles with the index
                                        and the little finger doesn't stop.
Across the base of the fingers, draw an arc.
A boat overturned this morning in the bay. What can a hand
                                                            be made to hull? What
all over the waves. Shade in the curve, in the hollow of the hand
where vision gets thin; whereas, from the back
one can see the tendons retrace, running parallel
to the swimmers, who by then are also lost, like the ribs
of a paper umbrella or lantern or any number of other things not nearly so fragile.

FINGERTIPS

In an x-ray you can tell
there's an interior nail, a glitch of bone that senses hold
                                                            a thousand
and then we were one,
or
then there was only one, and that was someone else. Attention can hone
down that close, and then the bone flattens out
just a bit
and you can hear
what it hears, and you can hear
it.

THE HAND: LOWER VIEW: OBLIQUE

Beveled from both
the dorsal and palmar approach: crisp machine of needle-bone, born to drift
                                        horizon-ward through the hollow world
wafts an invisible globe,
on a glass spine. The hand is a wheel
that comforts none. Be mine.

Attains an apse. Here, where a hasp is taking place
                                        into shape
                                        into gradual sense
                                                                        we ascend
"To that point, which in sum" or "Once, here was a hand."
An arch is necessarily geological   thus it ages; thus it ends. My friend
had a hand that wouldn't stop. My reign
of belief that says, "If a bevel,
then a dirigible" (which was not here before).

KNUCKLES

free of muscles, most closely resemble
the sun. Socket and phalanx
                                        lock
                                              the dome
and slip the light, diagonal
through a chambered nautilus
toward home, wherein
you can see through the skin, when it grips and goes white

and reads like a face, so many faces
line the body, or are lined up inside the body, waiting.

THE THUMB: BASED ON

the basal joint, permitting half
to that account
add one
gentle swan from the neck up. This enables reaching
and can only begin
to map what will eventually become
a circular man. Michelangelo gave the thumb a brain rooted in opposition. In fact, those born with more than one were considered blessed, and heaven would swing down within reach, while a sixth finger (or rather, technically, the fifth) was the devil's flesh. If it lived, it caused, and caught on things in passing, but they still passed.

THE INTERN'S PROBLEM

When a baby is born with six fingers (each one wanted and wanted to be
equally perfect) a young man
cuts off the withered excesses and wonders if he'll be sued
if what becomes
a blinking wing and/or why this road
suddenly clears.
Why does everything come in shards and a body is a body until it's cut. Sculpted
only doors that shut. One is forced to admit
that an infant belongs to no one.

In this case, however, the mother just laughed and pointed to the scars along her own ulnar edges. Extra fingers, it seems, can be removed to a certain extent.

THE THUMB, IN SUM

cannot touch the fingers; the fingers
must bend down to touch it   to bow from the waist
the average length   allows it to reach   each
                finger intact in the shadows it forms:
                        the tail of a bird,
                        a ship
below the horizon; it can barely dip
to the heart-line. A star that never quite rises
is measured by reflected light, that glow in the sky, the thumb
never entirely sets.

i.e., palmward and pulseward heading,

in the following order

we notice

that the bases of no two fingers touch, that

the bases of the fingers cannot touch the wrist, that the thumb

can only touch with its tip, and that in fewer places than it cannot

fold. Though you'd never describe it

as folding. You'd use the word 'following,' composed of

one non sequitur after another, and how soon we arrive at a century,

or any

one wanders from one's self every morning,

and continually as the day continues, and this is as it should be.

THE HAND: BACK VIEW, FINGERS ARCHED

Each lone slight arc
morticed and
threshold me home
to a slight curve in nature
as every bone in the body is barely
an arrow, all look out the window
onto passing umbrellas,
each flying buttress, a hand
is a standing wave.

As with the foot or the cathedral,
the arches cross each other rising
to the final finger and finer
high wire into
lofted thought, as they say of planes, and the analogy
is apt — the distinct angle of the bank, the giddiness of height
is grist
for the aerial earth: ridge and plain and potential signs of life.

THE FIST

In utter moon, this “we” is tool and when
a weapon is a closed thing
it’s not all that surprising

that it drives itself to dust. A radius of pain
that turns away (that grinds its face) that
bag of rain.

Note the singular. Has endless fingers, filters senses, running its appendages
through the sky, distracted,
                                        if you hold up
the hand in bright daylight, it is well known

that if you hold a flashlight behind the hand,
                                        palmar view,
                                in the dull red
                        you can see for miles and things
don't get smaller in the distance.

THE MECHANICS OF THE HAND

From the four corners of the wrist
flows the hand
In clasping bends
bends back
its whispered circle
labyrinth seed
whose broken hill
constitutes a system, adopted

this vagrant nation, tendon, and nerve
bends back
more easily into the world.

SIX American Sign Language

for Bay Anapol

SIGNS

Come back to their animals

                holding a black veil against a white wall
which, too, you can see through
the ornamented air
pared back.   My ghost migration engraved, stations
                of the
brightly map. We tag the wings
                                and in the slip that checks and graces,
little steeples that mean.

Sculpts. Just look at these neighbors. Who sees with the fingers
sees these things together. I once built a neighbor of light.
We used to read by his skin, the whole town, reciting, "Repeat after

until we could decipher branches signing in the storm and
long past the fields now speaking, walking on his hands out of town.

Think of the space in front of the body. You can't walk in. You can't find the door. We call it the present. You don't know what to do with your hands. Whereas the past is an orchard. This is how you know the difference. Birds live in orchards but not deer. This happens behind the body.

While everything in front is overexposed or snow. You stop at the edge and wave your arms, but they get lost in the wash of diffused light, which makes it the future. You are waving goodbye.

Point to an imaginary place. It need not be specific, but huge
areas are indicated and tend

no one ends

in a streak or flare. Location, which is not

exactly position each time you mention

several people form a field but must

relinquish their names at the edges; fraying *is* the body. It's just a semantic problem. A field of wheat and above it, an entire wind of bees. Take my picture. Please put the sun in the background and make it look like the wheat completely (remember several people can be discussed at once if you treat them as points in space).

THINKING AND FEELING

For instance, happy. That's far away. So we gesture a little to the right of the head
                                        is the sensation of
I couldn't say.
                        A chime in a cell.
You crave

none of these.

We place
                        an inch and a half behind your left shoulder
a bird the size of a thumbtack.
You have to keep it happy forever.

FLOOD

Make the hand a shell   saved along a sea
one sill at a time   the hands rise
and alight   from their eyelids every morning, place the open hands in front.
And the palms rise, and the tides, both
flora and fauna become inextricable
as you place both hands out, slightly cupped
until they overflow and here we stand convinced. We were hoping to be convinced.

GARDEN

The body is a circle, which comes home in the hands. Move
out and within it
                                        are the phyla; orbit these
                                                                (and if a sphere)
                                                                (this can also be invited)
                                                                            to pool in air
all gardens are equal parts water and beyond that
make a "yet"
                              with the right hand flowering. Plant it
and beyond that, keep planting the hands in increasing circles.

RAIN

This one is complicated. You'll need a lot of hands.
You're advised to prepare them in advance.
In front of you there will be a great water. Divide by two and bring together

the tips of the fingers, which
almost reach the earth, that is, they spread out from here and

Hold this (here you may insert any living object, just

use the left hand to soften the fingers of the right and sift, still softly, back and forth.

GHOST (HOLY)

Face the hands together face to face, right over left, leave

enough space.   There's a charge given off
                                                                                a field
                                                                                changed   a horizontal we
have a model in early Flemish landscape, all that sea, etc., all that sky or
in Millet's *Angelus* (1857) (form this with the left hand, the horizon turning gold)
          the right hand will move
off on its own, tremor, and skid into cloud. Certain moments
of indecision are visitations in disguise. It's this that lets
the hands pass at such incredible speed. Initialize these.

DEER

The slanted,
            though they prefer
roses, will settle
the bone tilted, will

                                        we

                                        of the have been, please place
at the eyebone, one or two thumbs, the hands
will do what they do most naturally they find
bone grows upward nine times out of ten.

EVENING

Arch the hand as if taking a pulse
on the wrong side of the wrist and let it hover. The other,
                                                                                    a dim crystal
                                                                                    transparent as early windows
were made of shell, shaved
                                        alabaster and mica, were moving
                                        evening
                                                    is a decimal, a subtle gradation toward
glass planes that become neither   more nor less an ocean or an empty
greenhouse in the dark: the often, sharpen, and there is no end
to the refraction, nor to the scattering of rays; i.e., we
who can see well at night are simply they who refuse to leave.

TO FORM THE SIMPLE PAST

If a glance over the shoulder implies we're going forward

like salt, row.

                                        Toward something behind
and the doors are all closed, and history peels
a fruit open to the mind. They say there's a past
that's simple as opposed to perfect. The ghost
just over the left shoulder also looks different
under the influence of human touch. You close it again
and it reduces like a fraction, something common
to every gesture, caught unaware. . . .

THE PRESENT PERFECT: TO HAVE

To have perfects the present: "to have laughed," "to have delved," "to have once
it was all of us. Your hands know this and automatically explode.
                                                            Proffer both — what they can do
to the self. And if the motion is absolute, it overflows its tense and is thus *is*
in the very sense
                        splits. With one hand on each side of the larynx,
point inward, my untoward angler, spelling "to hold" with your thumbs.

SUN

I've heard of people who've gone blind

who then begin to see with their skin;

it usually centers itself in the hands, the palms and the fingertips
most particularly, who
drive a car, who read the paper, who paint by number
in the sand, this sculpture, carved
                                        of instant substance
                                        is
                              the stated entrance; for instance,
the blind who sign find that air is a face.

ANIMAL

Place all fingertips on the skin of the chest in two neat lines and
arch, one above the heart; the other where no heart is, touch the skin
whenever possible
with bent hand
rocking
both hands sideways. Keep rocking.

SEVEN Shadow Puppets

THE FIRST MOVIES

Then all hands touched. Hands shone. The hand was a public thing.
A tool that rang when dropped. The two hands moved across
What moves between a screen and a match
awakened in the cold

(The smaller the light, the more enormous
the hands will live) by a sound
will be gone. Enormous trees, a castle, a pond
and no sky
in the broken ray
into birds on the opposite wall.

BIRDS

Most shadow puppets are birds. This all depends on darkness. Birds prefer darkness.
Cockatoo, parrot, and lark have in common
you can see through them; a density based on ambient light. They must live inside
any number of things. Things without number. Name them:
two flying birds
two flying birds
require both hands as
hands are more supple than the rest of the body
because they don't belong to it.

BIRDS

Behind frosted glass
grief shape

the finger tracing laterally
across the back of a mirror as you might, walking down a street
let your fingertip trail along the staves of passing gates
waist high
the birds dissolve,
brief lakes in the window of

Reflect thereon.
Therefore the reflected sun. The wound in my hand
aches in weather, any weather, tattooed all
the way up to the elbow. Now it's winter. Geese cross in their soft Vs, swift
sign in the cirrus. The hand writes in the air; the bird stays there.

BIRDS

Now you'll need thousands. Evenly though rapidly dispersed
every finger unfettered
                                        any bone
can be feathered, this thousand
                                        driven hollow
                        into the flock
                                    of all things numbered
one through one hundred. Never was I
so asunder, etc., so I
opened the window and let in the graves.

ADVANCES IN THE FORM

The latest work in shadow puppets is being done on verbs. Make the form of a soar, of a veer. Make the tense clear. Distinguish the past perfect from the simple past. Neither was. And on into conditionals. Would have found, etc. Would have gone
myself, but I wasn't home. Birdwatchers often use sign language because, though birds are fond of the human voice, they are downright hypnotized by the swaying hands and will walk right into them.

EIGHT A Manual of Gesture:

Public Speaking for the Gentleman (1879)

for Jena Osman

RIGHT HAND DESCENDING OBLIQUE PRONE

You lower the hand
more slowly
Yet rose (you say, gaze lowered)
                                        sweet dew, etc., to underscore the finality —
                                                    i.e., death is, etc., untimely
so begin by raising
the right hand slightly above the shoulder and then in a sweep
match
          the words; for instance, you wouldn't want to speak of heaven;
you'd find yourself facing backward, and all your ancestors
disconcertingly well prepared.

RIGHT HAND HORIZONTAL FRONT PRONE

Sometimes known as the “oncoming traffic pose,”
it must be accompanied by slightly glowering brow and glinting eye, which
stand in for the violins, etc.
                                        Lift off and adapt to emphatic speech
by bending slightly at the knee
as in the example: *“But*

                                                    the whole body angled forward.
                                                    There are
                                                                Hush!
                                                                Peace!
                                                                Seize!   the fleeing angel,

sacred, solemn, awe, or
the divine hand is upon you, is that curious thing
you might have noticed occurring on your shoulder.

RIGHT HAND ASCENDING LATERAL SUPINE

This, too, is for speaking of the sublime, but here we add the sacred and divide
by one. This
requires a practiced wrist. Practice
to avoid

from every mountain top, etc., shine

Of course you would.

And as the ascending stress arrives, the promontories repeat
the joy of, the glory of
the slightly cupped hand held out
as if testing for rain or thinking the weight
of an egg.

is highly recommended for dissuading ghosts (Oh! what is!
this darkness! etc.
coming from the east.   The hand goes one way, and the glance,
another, by natural magnetism shattered the challenge
and wept in gesture for nought (here look slightly up) "Be gone!" Begin
by sweeping the hand around from the back
in a wide arc; you can, in this way, imply everything in sight.

BOTH HANDS DESCENDING LATERAL PRONE

"Thou hast forgiven the iniquity of . . .
will encompass the wheel of what can be left
and then enter
the cast of thousands: the crowd moves in a shimmer
of heat over acres
thou hast covered all (emphasize
"covered" by extending your arms floorward, hands slightly splayed and face down
we hold back the rising flood
swelled to fill
an entire people marching toward

an avalanche of dust — *"My sons!"* and the hands are down, out flat, you sense
a pushing against the earth, and the earth pushing back. Wear a suit,
cite the numbers,
reveal your sources
(the manual says) (equalized
by the armload) If the fountain
heads downward, *"They forthwith do."* (Downplay the reverence;
it is clearly implied.)

NINE Paintings of Possible Hands

Wilton Diptych, 1395

"This is your dowry, O holy Virgin . . ."

          Ornate and absent: sky
while all the while
          How blue the robe
          How the blue robe
Here, wear blue, my
          you, my oh! look at their hands, too
immaculately long, no I mean, Look
at Mary's left hand, there's something
terribly wrong, though on second thought
perhaps it's an accident of light and even the hands
of the young king of England — the fingers innumerate — is just that something
slightly infinite in hands.

FRA ANGELICO, *Cell 7, San Marco*, 1438–43

Fra And
            of the Freed Hand
or of the hand in fore   of wristless air
where here the sky is greener,
full of hands that, alone, break down to lust
            are birds, all
lived twice, and this is his third
                                                fair acre,
                                                lover,
                                                only
                                                here
                                                they begin to emerge, hands first.

DOMINIQUE INGRES, *Venus at Paphos*, 1852–53

The hand, which is disappearing
                                        on the forearm finding
the child's fingers multiplying
          the child's feathered fingers
          or: the child's fingers are feathers
and the left hand of Venus
and the whole left arm, which
we can see through   (rather unnerving)
                    is a ghost
that is also not (yet) part of the child.

AUGUSTE RODIN, *Cathedral*, 1908

Nested dolls.
Heart, hand, and larger churches
forget to intend anything beyond. There is no door
to the room; it has been replaced by a room.

MARC CHAGALL, *Self-Portrait with Seven Fingers*, 1912

On the left hand
six fingers and a thumb
is to do it well.
is to do it without turning around. In the living air between heaven and hell
it's the sort of miracle that does no one any good. I count
with no reason, no object, I mean
that there is nothing counted.

MARCEL DUCHAMP, *Portrait of Doctor Raymond Dumouchel*, 1910

Huge and
Shake. It will be a little gift.
What is:
1. glows
2. is
what in the night sky seems
too green and keeps us up all night. My mask
walks. Walk on. We are walking east. *What hand?* his own notes said
what is that hand doing in the dark   we're all folded across
the huge red earth and here is my friend.

REMBRANDT VAN RIJN, *The Anatomy Lesson of Dr. Nicholaes Tulp*, DETAIL, 1632

He is cutting off a glove.
A million leaves. Though the eyes of everyone watching are simply black dots,
you can trace
their precise
sight-lines
they are
nothing I tell you he is cutting off a glove.

(Upper left corner. It appears incidental. It looks like a glove. It looks like he's going to cut off a glove.)

tossed his gloves on the table as he entered, they said

There is so much else going on. There are people taking notes,
others mapping veins. The gloves are white. And this seems, just for an instant,
cruel to them.

NORMAN BLUHM AND FRANK O'HARA, *Hand*, 1960

So much for the hills
          that still their animal time. To geometrize
in long, articulated lines. The hand upon the world
bends down and down and down.   "Meet me in the park." Embryonic
in its internal stair
                              conch
                                        vetch
                                                  what
                                                  tastes itself in sun
                                                  will not climb down.

SEAN SCULLY, *Landline Sand*, 1999

Now I dream them.
They have no paint. They are completely raw in that way.
Just bands of anchor or in the etchings
just black and white and itinerant greys.
I send you this effort when I meant the gesture.
Every abstract is a painting of yet another
(never repeated) part of the body.

KUHL HOUSE POETS

David Micah Greenberg *Planned Solstice*

John Isles *Ark*

Bin Ramke *Airs, Waters, Places*

Bin Ramke *Matter*

Michelle Robinson *The Life of a Hunter*

Robyn Schiff *Worth*

Cole Swensen *The Book of a Hundred Hands*

Cole Swensen *Such Rich Hour*

Emily Wilson *The Keep*